A BIRDWATCHING GUIDE TO

MENORCA, IBIZA & FORMENTERA

GW00683464

GRAHAM HEARL

With illustrations by
JOHN BUSBY

ARLEQUIN

ISBN 1 900159 20 1

First published 1996

Arlequin Press, 26 Broomfield Road, Chelmsford, Essex CM1 1SW
Telephone: 01245 267771
© Graham Hearl

All rights reserved. No part of this book may be reproduced, stored in a retrieval system or transmitted in any form or by any means, electronic, mechanical, photocopying or otherwise, without the permission of the publisher.

A catalogue record for this book is available.

Contents

Acknowledgements 4
General Introduction 6

Introduction Menorca 7
Birding Sites in Menorca 12
   S'Albufera es Grau 12
   Salinas de Montgofre (Addaia Salinas) 17
   Cap de Cavalleria and Tirant 19
   Cala Algaiarens 21
   Punta de s'Escullar 22
   Algendar Gorge 22
   Son Bou Marsh 24
   Other Sites 29

Introduction Ibiza 31
Birding sites in Ibiza (Eivissa) 34
   Las Salinas (Salinera Espanola) 34
   The west coast 35
   The north coast 36
   The east and south-east coast 37

Introduction Formentera 39
Birding sites in Formentera 41
   Estany Pudent and Salinas Marroig and Ferrer 41
   Estany des Peix and Es Estanyets .43
   Cap de Barbaria 43
   La Mola 43

   Other Sites 44
   Isla Espalmador and Isla Espardel .44
Other Flora and Fauna in Menorca and the Pitiusas 45
References 45
Checklist of the Birds of Menorca and the Pitiusas 46

Acknowledgements

For Menorca many thanks to Judy Edward and the Travel Club of Upminster.

For Ibiza many thanks to Roma Parmenter for organising the first trip; Bosky, Patsy and 'Ibosim' at San Antonio who took me to the Bledas Islands; Janice Sealey and Matheus Woldhuis at Es Cana for their marvellous hospitality; many thanks to David Coleman for his knowledge of Formentera; Tony Baker and 'Balmerino' who enabled me to get to the island of Espalmador; Derek Moore who came to my rescue with photographs of S'Albufera es Grau, Menorca when I had a disaster with my camera, and last but definitely not least, to my wife Irene who produced the site maps.

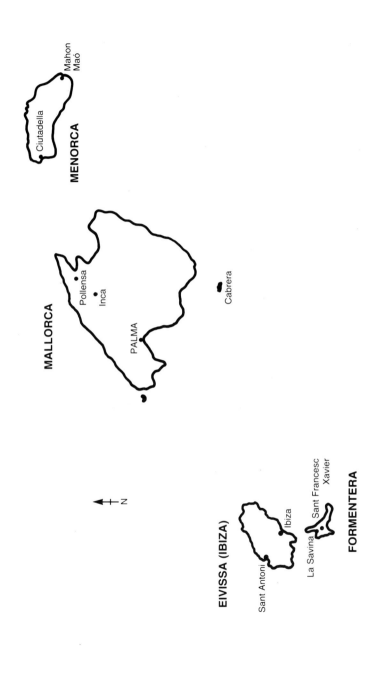

Map 1. The Balearic Islands showing the principal towns and relative position of each island

MENORCA

Mahon
Maó

Ciutadella

MALLORCA

Pollensa

Inca

PALMA

Cabrera

N

EIVISSA (IBIZA)

Sant Antoni

Ibiza

La Savina

Sant Francesc
Xavier

FORMENTERA

5

General Introduction

The Balearic Islands are important staging posts for migrants crossing the Mediterranean; Mallorca is the best known of these islands and has been a popular destination for birdwatchers over the years since the seventies enabling birdwatchers from northern Europe to get their first knowledge of Mediterranean species and experience the impressive migration; the authoritative birdwatching guide to Mallorca has already been published in this series (A Birdwatching Guide to Mallorca by Graham Hearl and Jon King).

This guide covers the smaller lesser known islands of the Balearics, Menorca and the Pitiusas, i.e. Ibiza and Formentera. All three of these islands are well known as holiday destinations, especially Ibiza, but all are not well known ornithologically, except as seabird breeding areas, and their potential as birdwatching holiday destinations has not been fully explored, this guide therefore details sites and areas worth exploring for birds in these islands.

It is possible to travel between the islands as they are interconnected by air and sea routes, but only through Mallorca, you cannot travel direct from Menorca to Ibiza for instance.

A checklist of the birds of Menorca and the Pitiusas is included towards the back of this book; as Menorca is separated from the Pitiusas by some 190.0 km the avifauna shows considerable variations from island to island and from Mallorca, (for example Black Vulture is a resident on Mallorca but has only very occasionally been recorded on Menorca; and Rock Sparrow, a rare migrant and very occasional breeding bird on Mallorca, is resident on Ibiza and Formentera), the checklist endeavours to give the differing status for the islands but reference must be made to the text for the local status and is described in much more detail in the forthcoming publication by T. & A.D. Poyser, 'Birds of the Balearic Islands' (King J. and Hearl G.C. in prep.).

The GOB and submitting records

All the islands have their own local branch of the Balearic conservation bird group called by the acronym GOB (Grup Balear d'Ornitologia i Defensa de la Naturalesa), now one of Spain's largest non-governmental conservation organisations, with the aim of the conservation of the natural environment of the Balearics. All visiting birdwatchers are able to help the increasing knowledge about birds in these islands by forwarding their bird records to Graham Hearl, Apartado 83, Sa Pobla, Mallorca.

Using this guide

There are two languages in use in the Balearics, Spanish (Castellano) and dialects of Catalan, slightly different in each island; consequently you will sometimes find different names and spellings used on various maps and signposts for some of the sites, these alternatives are given in parentheses where relevant. For example one of the most common variations is the use of the Catalan 'Eivissa' for Ibiza and 'Maó' for Mahon and more modern maps and signposts will use the Catalan form; however I have used Ibiza as most people will know the island and town by this name and likewise with Mahón.

Any tourist road map of the Balearics will enable you to find the sites detailed in this guide, the Firestone map of the Balearics E-56 being a good example.

Menorca

Introduction Menorca

Menorca is much smaller than it's sister island Mallorca, being only 48.0 km from east to west and 19.0 km from north to south. It does not possess any high mountains like Mallorca but, having a greater rainfall, it presents a much gentler and greener landscape with low rolling hills and farmland. Much of the farmland is given over to grass and cattle, with the fields surrounded by stone walls but not enclosing the fig and almond trees so typical of Mallorca.

The main road runs from Ciutadella in the west to Mahon in the east cutting the island in two halves, rolling hills to the north and the wooded 'barrancos' or steep gorges to the south.

Menorca has always maintained a lower profile than it's more brash neighbours of Mallorca and Ibiza, the atmosphere is very relaxed and the pace much slower, and development has been kept reasonably under control except in one or two locations. Nonetheless the infrastructure is in place to cater for the holiday maker with flights available from many airports in the UK direct to Mahon (Maó), and many travel agents offer package deals to Menorca.

It is also very easy to combine a few days birding on Menorca with a birdwatching holiday to Mallorca; a ferry service has recommenced between Puerto Alcudia on Mallorca and Ciutadella on Menorca. The ferry can take cars as well as just foot passengers and runs daily throughout the year. Birdwatching from the ferry is excellent and you will be right in amongst Cory's and Mediterranean Shearwaters for most of the three hour trip; you may even see Dolphins as well which regularly pass between the islands.

Enquiries can be made either through your travel agent, direct with the ferry company or local travel agents when you are in Mallorca; you will presumably be staying in the north-east of Mallorca in any case where Puerto Alcudia is situated.Should you not like boat trips, you can fly instead with regular flights throughout the day from Palma. Mallorca to Mahon for about £50.00 return.

Accomodation can be booked in advance, but at the birding times of spring and autumn there should be little difficulty in finding accommodation should you decide to go on the spur of the moment.

Birds in Menorca and when to stay

The birdwatching is a little different from Mallorca, there is less local shooting on Menorca and the birds certainly appear tamer and much more confiding. There are certain areas that are a must for the birdwatcher but they are distributed around the island and not concentrated in any one area, in fact any area you happen to be in will be rewarding as regards birdwatching especially keeping one eye on the sky for raptors that can occur anywhere, anytime.

The resident Balearic specialities such as Audouin's Gull, Black-winged Stilt, Sardinian Warbler, Blue Rock Thrush and Thekla Lark are here, the latter in very good numbers; Pallid Swift breed in various colonies around the coast, and the island is especially good for seeing Egyptian Vulture, Red Kite and Booted Eagle, all these raptors being easier to see here than anywhere else in the Balearics.

Another interesting resident is the Dartford Warbler, this species, a winter visitor to Mallorca and originally to Menorca as well, stayed to breed on Menorca in 1980 and has since displaced the once resident Marmora's Warbler; they are mainly to be found on the north coast but are nowhere common on the island. The island is also a stronghold for Cory's Shearwater, most of the major colonies in the Balearics are on the north coast of Menorca; the Mediterranean race of Shag *Phalacrocorax aristotelis desmarestii*. also breeds around the coast.

Menorca in conjunction with the other islands in the group has a good passage of migrants especially in spring and to a lesser extent in autumn, therefore the ideal time to visit is from early-April to mid-May combining resident species with migrants. With good wetland areas in winter holding wildfowl and wintering waders, an out of season holiday could be rewarding, but should you wish to come in high season there are always the summer residents such as Bee-eaters to enthral you.

Menorca in winter, apart from holding wildfowl such as Wigeon, Shoveler, Teal, Mallard, and waders such as Woodcock and Snipe, also plays host to passerines escaping from the cold northern European climate, and species such as Song Thrush, Robin, Black Redstart are here in numbers as well as Redwing, Fieldfare and Mistle Thrush in lesser quantities.

Spring is always the most popular time for birders; in early spring, passage migrants combined with many wintering species provide a substantial varied list; and later in spring the summer visitors have replaced the wintering birds including the arrival of Bee-eaters, a much more abundant summer breeding bird here than on Mallorca and the other islands.

Return migration starts in July with returning waders but is in full swing late August /early September and continues into October, but, as with the rest of the Balearics, in not such spectacular fashion as in spring but always well worth experiencing.

Where to stay

Menorca is the perfect holiday destination for the birdwatcher who prefers a more relaxed and quieter holiday, there are far fewer birdwatchers to contend with than on Mallorca where they are concentrated in the one area in the north-east of the island, especially in spring. It also provides an ideal combined birdwatching/family holiday location as all the birding sites are within easy reach wherever you are staying on the island, and nearly all are next to gorgeous beaches or calas. There is therefore no recommended centre to stay on the island, anywhere that takes your fancy will put you in touch with the birds and keep your family happy although one or two places do have a slight advantage for the birder.

Son Bou, situated on the south coast, is a popular holiday resort with a variety of accommodation from hotel to self catering; the vista of all the buildings is not ideal but you would be able to cover the excellent Son Bou marsh before breakfast, before the sunbathers get out on the beach and before you travel to quieter birding areas.

Anywhere on the east coast would put you closer to the wader spots such as the Albufera es Grau or Fornells, but the author's favourite is Cala Galdana, a beautiful if overdeveloped cala on the south coast, BUT, right at the base of the spectacular Algendar Gorge, ideal for that early morning or evening walk to check for any new migrants.

Food and shopping

As in the other Balearic islands self-catering is a popular option for birdwatchers giving more flexibility over meal times. All the main towns now have supermarkets which are open from 8.00 am to 1.00 pm and again from 4.00 pm to 8.00 pm. There is not the enormous range of local bars in inland towns compared to Mallorca but all the resorts cater well for the visitor and, if you look, you will find bars and restaurants serving local cuisine as well as others serving the more usual holiday beefburger and chips fare. The country restaurants are especially recommended and most are well advertised locally.

Getting around

Virtually every resort will have one worthwhile birdwatching site or good birdwatching area within walking distance but, for the birdwatcher intending to cover the best sites, hiring a car is essential as most of the best birding spots are off the main roads away from public transport. The road system on Menorca is rather like a fish bone i.e. a main spine road, from Mahon to Ciutadella, with side roads and tracks leading off; it is not easy to do a circular route except in the east of the island. Car hire is readily available and reasonably cheap and the driving is easy (taking care to drive on the right,of course) although some of the side roads can get rather narrow with bad surfaces, especially if you start to explore some of the narrower back tracks. It is worth mentioning here that a lot of the tracks are gated; this used to mean on Menorca that you could open the gate and drive through, but it is now best to stop and get permission before entering, especially where the notices are new and explicit; or except where instructed in the site information, which, of course, is always subject to change.

You need to carry your driving license (the pink, European driving license as issued in the UK) and passport when using a hire car. The wearing of seat belts is compulsory at all times and random breath tests are used. Petrol is approximately the same price as in the UK and most towns have a petrol station.

There is public transport available on the island but this would not prove very efficient for the birdwatcher as only the main towns and resorts are covered. Likewise the island does not lend itself to coverage by bicycle for the birdwatcher as the sites are widespread and, despite having no mountains, a lot of hills and distance are involved.

Weather and clothing

Menorca has more rainfall than Mallorca and can certainly be a lot windier, therefore it is best to be prepared for all conditions, certainly if contemplating a holiday at the usual best birdwatching times of spring and autumn when the weather is at it's most variable. Temperatures at these times can vary from just a few degrees with rain to well up into the twenties so pack woollies and waterproofs as well as the shorts and suntan lotion.

Crime

Menorca has not, so far, suffered as much as Mallorca and Ibiza from theft from tourist cars, but it would certainly be sensible not to leave any valuables in the vehicle unattended even for a short while as it is only inviting theft. As in all tourist areas it is best to be sensible with your valuables by keeping hotel rooms locked and making use of hotel safes where available.

Other general points

The money unit is the peseta, now worth about 200 to the pound sterling, and you will be able to change money, cash and travellers cheques at hotels, travel agents, and many shops; but the rates offered are often slightly poorer than those found in banks which are only open in the mornings.

The native language on Menorca is Menorquin, (a dialect of Catalan) but Spanish (Castellano) is spoken by all the islanders, and in all the coastal resorts English is understood by most people who are connected with the tourist industry such as in hotels, shops and restaurants; a phrase book, however, is always useful.

There are no poisonous snakes or scorpions on the island to worry about but when birding in the wetter habitats you may encounter mosquitoes at certain times of the year and should you react to bites the use of a suitable insect repellent is advisable.

Finally please bear in mind that details of sites and, more particularly, access to sites is subject to change.

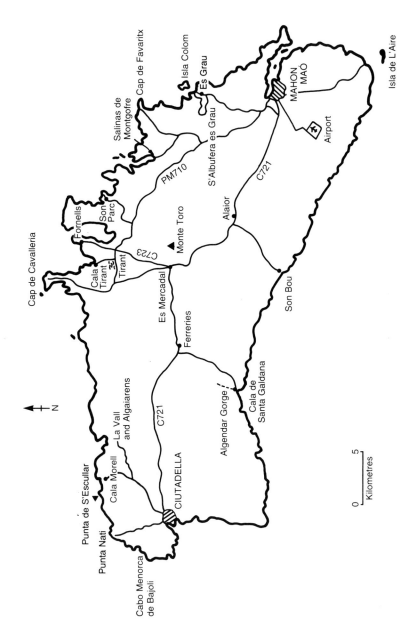

Map 2 The island of Menorca showing principal roads, towns and birdwatching sites.

Punta de S'Escullar
Punta Nati
Cabo Menorca de Bajoli
Cala Morell
La Vall and Algaiarens
CIUTADELLA
C721
Algendar Gorge
Cala de Santa Galdana
Ferreries
Es Mercadal
Son Bou
Cala Tirant
Tirant
Fornells
Son Parc
C723
Monte Toro
Cap de Cavalleria
PM710
S'Albufera es Grau
Alaior
C721
Salinas de Montgofre
Cap de Favaritx
Isla Colom
Es Grau
MAHON MAÓ
Airport
Isla de L'Aire

N

0   5
Kilometres

11

Birding sites in Menorca

Map 3. S'Albufera es Grau, Menorca.

S'Albufera es Grau (Map 3)

S'Albufera es Grau is the only official reserve on Menorca and consists of a large brackish lake (Plate 1) and surrounding garigue areas amounting to 1,887 ha of which the wet area is 67 ha, some of the small bays on the inland end of the lake are backed by small reedbeds and sedge (see Plate 2). A large development and golf course called Shangri La (Plate 3) adjoining and overlooking the south side of the lake was started in the early eighties, but the local conservation group GOB Menorca and others were concerned about the impact that this large development would have and they campaigned successfully to have the area declared a Parc Naturel in May 1995 but the development had been halted some years before this date. There are still scattered villas in the area but the golf course is now in decline and most of the tracks that were bulldozed through for the road system have never been surfaced. These tracks are still mostly passable by car but the ones closer to the lake are now being closed to traffic; it is still possible to walk these tracks which, in places, give good views over the inland portion of the lake and some of the bays which attract waders.

   To get there take the PM 710 road from Mahon towards Fornells, about 1.0 km from Mahon turn right on the road to Es Grau, the entrance to Shangri La is 3.8 km along this road. Continue towards Es Grau to K6.0, just before the resort of Es Grau, here there is a small parking area for no more than four cars but it is possible to park on the road as it is quite wide at this point with a lay-by. Alternatively continue the short distance to the beach at Es Grau , park and walk back or walk round the bay and out onto the headland.

   ❶At K6.0 the entrance to the reserve area is on your left marked with a new green

Plate 1. *S'Albufera es Grau, Menorca, a general view of the lake and the surrounding scrub.*

Derek Moore

Plate 2. *S'Albufera es Grau, Menorca, the reedbed at the west inland end of the lake.*

Derek Moore

Plate 3. *Shangri La, es Grau, Menorca, the development before it was halted, the remnants of the golf course can be seen on the right, with a glimpse of the lake in the background.*

Derek Moore

Plate 4. *Salinas de Montgofre, Menorca, showing the scrub margins and small disused pans ideal for waders and wagtails, and the sandy area at the back where Bee-eaters are often seen.*

Graham Hearl

Plate 5. *Cap de Cavalleria, Menorca, showing the fields and scrub in the foreground leading to the barren cape up to the lighthouse, this area is ideal habitat for Thekla Lark and Stone Curlew.*

Graham Hearl

Plate 6. *Cap de Cavalleria, Menorca, and the Port de Sanitja, the haunt of Osprey with the island of Sanitja in the background.*

Graham Hearl

Plate 7. *Tirant, Menorca, the flat area at the back of Cala Tirant showing the typical low rolling hills of the northern part of the island; when flooded, this area attracts waders and wildfowl in winter.*

Graham Hearl

Plate 8. *Algendar Gorge, Menorca, one of the best migration spots on the island and showing the cliffs which are the haunt of Red Kite and Egyptian Vulture.*

Graham Hearl

sign 'S'Albufera Es Grau'; at the moment there is no reception nor any marked tracks or hides.

Access to the eastern and northern side of the lake is via a track and footpath from the small parking area at K6.0; take this track, which is barred to vehicles by a chain, go round the locked gates and over the small stone bridge, check here for Kingfisher, ahead is the lake itself.

The path bears round to the right and forks 50 m on, the left fork takes you up to a mound ❷, it is quite a steep overgrown path but the view from the top over the lake is a good vantage point for scanning for duck, gulls and terns.

The right fork is the main path and bears round through a small pine wood, check the woods for Hoopoe, Firecrest, Crossbill and, in spring, Golden Oriole as well as warblers. Approximately 250 m on, the path emerges into a clearer area, here you can take a smaller side path to the left through a small but obvious gap between a stone and concrete bollard, follow this sandy track up to where it overlooks the lake and one of the small bays.

❸ Approach the top of the rise with care so you can scan the bay to the right for waders such as Common and Wood Sandpiper before you disturb them; ahead are the two small hills or mounds seen from the path when you first enter the reserve area, the path continues up onto these mounds and from here you get a good clear view over most of the lake from the eastern side, ideal in the morning with the sun behind you. There are narrow paths meandering round the two mounds so pick a suitable spot and scan the lake for grebes, duck, gulls, marsh terns and, of course, the raptors such as Red Kite, Osprey, Booted Eagle and Kestrel. In winter the lake holds large concentrations of duck including Greylag Geese as well as Cormorants and a large roost of Starling.

Following the path to the right round the right-hand mound takes you round the north side of the lake, it is possible to follow this path for some considerable distance but the path is stony and follows the edge of the lake and, depending on the season, might be wet or even covered with water.

Alternatively return to the main path and continue on up to the headland ❹ overlooking the island, Isla Colom, looking for Thekla Lark as well as Sardinian Warbler and Shag offshore.

To cover the area thoroughly return to the road and take the Shangri La turn off ❺, continue straight ahead until the tarmac finishes and continue on the track until you reach the green 'S'Albufera es Grau' sign, from here you will probably have to walk to explore the old tracks scanning the lake for terns and duck when the views allow ❻ and ❼.

❽ Try and get to the western end by following the tracks to where you get a good view over the reed and sedge area at the inland end of the lake.

It is easy to loose you sense of direction in this maze of roads and tracks, but don't worry too much you will eventually find your way out, I always do; but DO allow sufficient time and daylight in case you lose your way.

Salinas de Montgofre (Addaia Salinas) (Map 4)

These old salt pans are situated at the southern inland end of the Addaia inlet and are on a private estate, access is only on foot and it is best to write for permission to enter prior to your visit; write to La Fundación Rubió-Tuduri Andrómaco, Calle Costa de sa Placa, Maó, Menorca or Fax 35 21 60.

This is a superb area of old disused pans very attractive to waders and Flamingos and approached through a very picturesque valley with unusual rock formations.

To get there take the PM 710 road from Mahon to Fornells and at K9.0 turn off right to Cap de Favaritx, at 2.1 km on this road take a left turn down an unmade road opposite green metal gates with a sign 'Morella Vell' and follow this road for 2.5 km until you reach the gates to the Montgofre estate signed 'Montgofre Nou' and 'propriedad privado' ❶; these gates may or may not be closed, but park here outside the gates and walk in to the salinas.

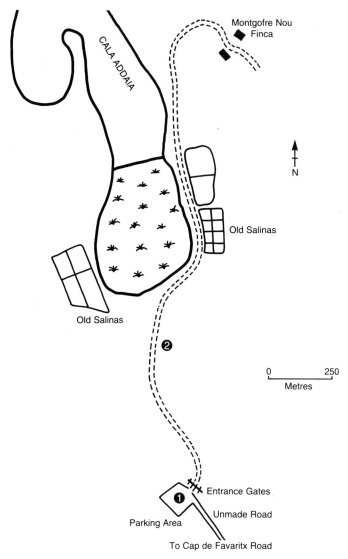

Map 4. Salinas de Montgofre, Menorca.

This road from the Cap de Favaritx road is marked as a through road on most maps but there is a 'no through road' or 'cul de sac' sign at the start of the road which is the correct situation.

The road to the estate gates where you park passes through very attractive scenery of small hills and limestone/sandstone rocky outcrops with small areas of woodland, all most suitable for the birds of prey for which Menorca is famous so it is recommended to stop and scan the area frequently. In fact the whole area from the main road to the Cap de Favaritx was formerly a wetland drained by the British in the eighteenth century and remnants of tamarisks and reeds still remain.

From the gates to the estate approach the salinas ❷, approximately 500 m, with care to avoid flushing the birds, the salinas are on either side of the road; do not leave the road as you are on private land. Birds to be seen here can include most sandpipers including Marsh and Wood Sandpiper as well as the more usual Black-winged Stilt, Kentish and Little-ringed Plover; Flamingos are also regular here and the area is also well suited to Bee-eaters (see Plate 4). The best birdwatching is all around this area of old salinas at the southern end of the Addaia inlet, so, even with your applied permission and letter, it is suggested that you do not proceed further than the first bend up the hill where it approaches the Montgofre Nou Finca.

Return to the road and continue on for 5.0 km to Cap de Favaritx, scanning the roadsides for Tawny Pipit, Short-toed Lark and the usual Stonechat and Hoopoe as you go. At the cape, there is a most spectacular barren almost moonscape area of black shale with virtually no vegetation, and from here you can scan the sea for flocks of shearwaters and Shag.

Returning from Cap de Favaritx, after 1.0 km from the end, take a dirt road on the left and go down the track for another 1.0 km, park and take a footpath on the left which will bring you to a beach, the Platja de Capifort, with a small lake to the right. The lake is good for water birds and maybe even a Marsh Harrier; even though it may be dry in summer the area is still good for Thekla Lark and even Dartford Warbler although this species is rare despite having ousted the Marmora's Warbler on Menorca.

There may be locked gates at the start of the dirt road so take heed of the current situation and walk from here if necessary.

Cap de Cavalleria and Tirant (Map 5)

These two distinct areas are described together due to their close proximity.

The Tirant wetland is situated just south of Cala Tirant and is a low area of tamarisk and rushes that dries in summer but has water for most of the autumn, winter and spring after seasonal rain.

The Cap de Cavalleria (Plate 5) is another marvellous peninsular totally different from the Cap de Favaritx, and is the most northerly point on Menorca; the scenery is outstanding and the area holds Stone Curlew, Thekla Lark, Short-toed Lark, Tawny Pipit and Spectacled Warbler, also an Osprey is frequently to be seen fishing in the Port de Sanitja.

Cap de Cavalleria

To get there take the first turning left into Mercadal if coming from Ciutadella. In Mercadal take the fork signposted 'Playas Costa Norte', at 2.0 km out from Mercadal there is a new Depuradora (Water treatments works) on the right hand side and it is always worth scanning for waders and wagtails, after a further 1.0 km take a right fork signposted 'Cavalleria, Binimel La', another 2.5 km on at the tee junction with a stop sign turn left signposted 'Cavalleria, Binimel La and Pregonda' (you can turn right here to Tirant), after another 1.0 km there is a sign 'Cavalleria' on the right on gates to a track.

❶ Take this track, don't worry if the gates are shut just open and close behind you; there is a new access road under construction about 200 m further on so take whichever one is open to the Cap. The area is very open consisting of rolling pasture and fields before developing into very low scrub on the peninsular itself. There are a few gates to be opened, AND SHUT, on this track but there is no restriction of access to this wonderful area remember to stop and scan the surrounding fields on the way.

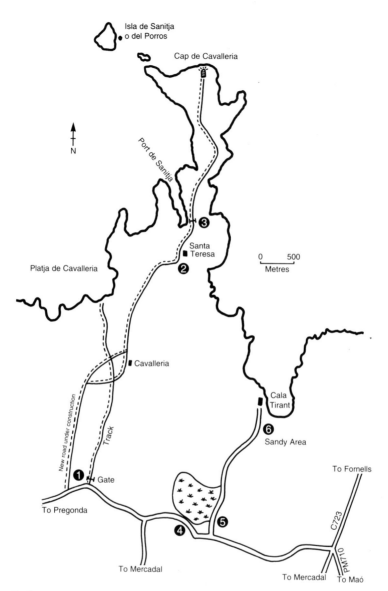

Map 5. Cap de Cavalleria and Tirant, Menorca.

After 1.4 km the track joins the new access, the farmhouse on the right is called Cavalleria; go straight on to get to the Cap again stopping to check the fields for larks, pipits and wheatears, after another 0.5 km the track goes on to the Playa de Cavalleria but turn right to get to the Cap.

❷ Another 2.0 km further on, where the track deteriorates at Santa Teresa, there is a wall and small stream, this is a nice wet area with tamarisks which attracts warblers and in winter and autumn attracts thrushes including Redwing and Fieldfare as well as wintering Serin and other finches.

After Santa Teresa carry on to the lighthouse signposted 'Faro', the vegetation now changes to low scrub, the cala on the left, called Port de Sanitja (Plate 6), attracts Osprey and it is probably worthwhile parking soon after the track passes through a pair of wooden gates ❸ to enjoy a walk to the lighthouse birding as you go for Stone Curlew, Thekla Lark and Dartford Warbler. At the lighthouse scan the sea for the expected shearwaters, Shag and Audouin's Gull.

Tirant

Return to the tee junction on the road from Mercadal and continue on for 0.5 km, on the left is a lowland wet area at the back of Tirant ❹, the amount of water varies dramatically and depends on the amount of recent rainfall and the time of year, in summer it will be practically dry but in spring and late autumn/winter the wet areas will be well worth scanning for waders and harriers both Marsh and Montagu's; marsh terns can also be found here depending on the water level and season. It is difficult to park here as the road is narrow so watch out for a suitable parking spot being careful not to block access to private property.

After another 1.0 km there is a left turn to Cala Tirant with, seen from the opposite direction, a white wall with a painted sign 'Cala Tirant', turn left here ❺, the variable wet area continues on your left hand side and this is a safer area to stop and park for scanning on both sides of the road; Plate 7 shows the view from this point and the extent of the wet area after rain.

❻ Further on this road approaching Cala Tirant there is a sandy area to the right which holds Bee-eaters in summer.

You can also approach Tirant from the main road C723 from Mercadal to Fornells; at the crossroads to Mahon at K5. 0 turn left and 2. 0 km from the crossroads you will come to the white wall on the Cala Tirant turn-off; and by continuing on towards Binimel La, Pregonda you will come to the turn-off to Cap de Cavalleria.

Algaiarens

The Algaiarens area is a beautiful valley and cala on the north coast favoured by Red Kite, Egyptian Vulture and Bee-eaters which inhabit the large, mainly disused sand quarry on the private estate of La Vall near Ciutadella. There is a controversy which has been running for some time between the locals and the estate about right of access, so until this is resolved it is best to enquire beforehand. The latest information on access is that it is open all the year from 10.00 am to 5.30 pm, cost of parking 500 pesetas, but it may be best to write to Seprome S.L., Placa des Born No.2, Ciutadella, Menorca, for permission, but don't assume automatic approval if you don't receive a reply.

To get there take the Cala Morell road north-east out of Ciutadella by turning left at the roundabout with the large bronze statue of a prancing horse on the Mahon road and follow signs to Cala Morell and Cala Algaiarens. Where the road turns off left for Cala Morell, after 5.0 km, carry straight on signposted 'La Vall' for another 2.5 km through pinewoods with stone walls on either side, don't forget to stop and scan at various places where you can park; this road will bring you down into the La Vall estate. The road is gated, signed 'propriedad privada' and there may well be a guard on the gate taking parking fees and or inspecting permission, if you gain access follow the walking track to the cala and explore the area around the car park and edges of the quarry.

The main attraction of the area is the large colony of Bee-eaters dispersed throughout the old quarry but the area is superb for the birds of prey, Red Kite, Booted Eagle and J Egyptian Vulture; Red-footed Falcon is also a good possibility.

The car park area gives a good open view for raptors, and Bee-eaters are always present in spring and summer

The quarry area has low sand mounds used by the Bee-eaters, plus Tawny Pipits Short-toed Lark and Woodchat Shrike; explore but be careful NOT to disturb any breeding birds especially the Bee-eaters.

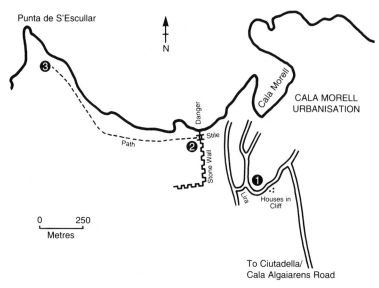

Map 6. Punta de s'Escullar, Menorca.

Punta de s'Escullar (Map 6)

This coastal point is just to the west of Cala Morell and is typical of the north-west coast of the island, very barren and very stony so good footwear is necessary to walk on the cliffs.

To get there take the road to Cala Morell out of Ciutadella following the road down into the cala from the Cala Algaiarens road, 7.5 km from Ciutadella to Cala Morell.

❶ At Cala Morell take the first turn on the left, street signposted 'Lira', just past the cave dwellings ; you will find horrible all white buildings in this urbanisation but the wonderful garigue area on the left is ideal for scrub species. Park on the left near the end of the street and cross over the very stony ground to the stone wall, there is a stone stile near the cliff end. ❷ Climb over the stile next to the sheer drop to the sea and from here follow a recognisable footpath west towards the point of Punta de s'Escullar ❸; if you wish, it is possible to walk from here all the way to Ciutadella around the coast.

The area is very barren but you will see typical birds of the coast such as Pallid Swift, Crag Martin, Blue Rock Thrush, Thekla Lark, Tawny Pipit and Spectacled Warbler as well as Wheatear, Black Redstart and Whinchat in spring and autumn. The real ornithological wealth of this area is the colony of Cory's Shearwaters, one of the largest in the western Mediterranean, these birds are best seen in the late afternoon when they approach the coast to return to their burrows when thousands can be seen along with a few Mediterranean Shearwaters; Shag and Yellow-legged Gull also breed on these cliffs.

Algendar Gorge (Map 7)

One of the best sites on the island and certainly one of the most spectacular. The gorge is typical of the barrancos of the southern coast of Menorca and one of the easiest to get into as far as birding goes. The habitat consists of lush vegetation in the valley bottom with a small stream, enclosed by high imposing limestone cliffs (Plate 8). These cliffs are the nesting habitat of Booted Eagle, Egyptian Vulture, Kestrel and Peregrine as well as Rock Dove and Blue Rock Thrush. The valley bottom has Nightingale, Cetti's Warbler and Moorhen nesting in the stream, and in October 1995 was alive with butterflies, Cleopatras, Painted Ladies, Bath Whites, Speckled Woods, Hummingbird Hawk Moths and Lang's Short-tailed Blue.

To get there take the turning off the C721 main Ciutadella/Mahon road at Ferreries, 8.0 km west of Mercadal, south to Cala de Santa Galdana.

Go straight across at the roundabout just before Cala Galdana and over the Torrente Algendar bridge. At the mini roundabout just after the bridge, turn right and drive to the end of this road, about 1.0 km, until you come to a pair of wooden gates, park here on

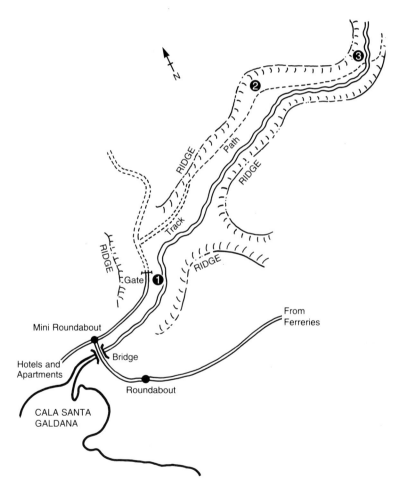

Map 7. Algendar Gorge, Menorca.

23

the right hand side, you are now at Algendar Gorge.

❶ The gated entry to the gorge has a private notice but at present you can ignore this, climb over the low wall (possible by all but the extreme infirm) to the right of the gate and you are in the Algendar Gorge.

After 100 m the track bends to the right and forks; straight on takes you up the side of the gorge and away from the valley bottom through pine wood until it emerges to typical coastal scrub where you may see the typical scrub species such as Sardinian Warbler and maybe Spectacled Warbler; a nice walk but the birds here are typical of Mediterranean Holm Oak and Pine woods.

The main track for birdwatchers bends right and continues to follow the valley bottom with the stream on your right-hand side, continue following this track and footpath for as far as you wish. The path passes Holm Oak Woods on your left with the open valley floor to your right, at another pair of wooden gates climb over by the wall on the left and follow the track which becomes a path skirting the edge of small fields under the cliffs, the valley floor is cultivated in small fields at this point but it is possible to pass round the edges of these fields.

❷ The valley opens out on the left to a very impressive rock face of sandstone and tufa, here is probably the best spot in the Balearics to watch out for Booted Eagle and Egyptian Vulture.

❸ Soon after, where the valley bends to the right and narrows, the path crosses the stream (approx. 2.0 km from the start), it is possible to cross the stream and continue further on up the gorge but the path now becomes very overgrown with brambles and the going is tough and difficult; however the best birding is lower down the gorge where it is wider and the views of birds of prey overhead not so fleeting.

If you are staying at Cala Galdana this walk makes an ideal daily pre-breakfast or evening walk looking out for migrants as well as the resident species.

Son Bou (Map 8)

This is the largest area of reedbed on the island, approx. 2.0 km long by 200 m wide extending inland at the western end, and sandwiched between the beach and dunes, and the holiday development of villas and apartments of Son Bou. It is an important area for migrants as well as breeding birds such as Cettis' Warbler and a small population of Moustached Warblers.

To get there take the turning off the C 721, the main Ciutadella/Mahon road at Alaior signposted 'Son Bou' and continue to the coast at Son Bou passing through the tunnel and past the old houses cut into the rock on the left side. Just past the Club Royal Son Bou take the left fork, go past the one high-rise hotel in Son Bou down to the beach and turn right into the beach car-park.

❶ At the end of the car park take a path at the left corner westward between the beach and the marsh scanning over the marsh for herons and Marsh Harriers, Moustached Warblers, Great Reed Warblers and other marsh birds as well as looking out for migrants such as wheatears, pipits and chats on the dunes; scan the sea also for terns, gulls and waders on the beach.

Just past a small house, 'La Casilla', the dunes open out to a bigger system and the marsh widens from the narrow strip and extends inland up into the barranco; just offshore here there is a small island worth scanning for shags, gulls and terns.

❷ Continue on to the small headland and search for wheatears and pipits; Plate 9 shows the reedbed extending inland into the barrancos with Son Bou to the right.

From the headland either return to the car park, or it is possible to continue and complete the circuit by heading inland but be prepared to climb one or two gates or walls. If the weather has been dry it will be possible to head inland between the marsh and a stone wall; if not, climb over the metal gate to the field in front of you and head

Plate 9. *Son Bou, Menorca, the reedbed taken from the coastal dunes with Son Bou in the background, this is the largest area of reeds on Menorca.*

Graham Hearl

Plate 10. *View from Monte Toro, Menorca, the highest viewpoint on Menorca and a good vantage point for raptors.*

Graham Hearl

Plate 11. *The Salinas, Ibiza, the best birding site on Ibiza viewed from the coast towards the airport with the western hills in the background. The only wetland area on Ibiza that attracts waders and especially Flamingos.*

Graham Hearl

Plate 12. *The islands of Es Vedra and Es Vedranella, Ibiza, a breeding site for Eleonora's Falcon.*

Graham Hearl

Plate 13. Estany Pudent, Formentera, this large area of water attracts waders and wildfowl as well as migrants around the fringes; La Savina is the town in the background.

Graham Hearl

Plate 14. Es Estanyets, Es Peix, Formentera, an area of disused saltpans at the western edge of Estany des Peix.

Graham Hearl

Plate 15. *Cap de Barbaria, Formentera, is even more barren than the La Mola area, but being the southernmost point on the Balearics it is the first landfall from Spain and Africa and can be alive with migrants in spring and autumn.*

Graham Hearl

Plate 16. *La Mola, Formentera, this eastern point of Formentera is very flat and barren but provides a good viewpoint for shearwaters and the ideal habitat for Rock Sparrow.*

Graham Hearl

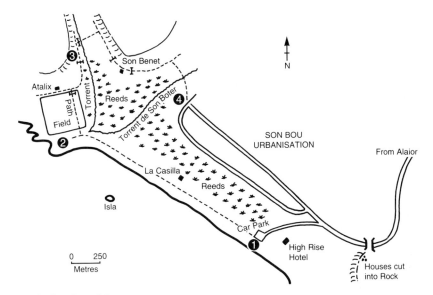

Map 8. Son Bou, Menorca.

---

inland on an obvious track across the field. At the end of the field go through the gate, shutting it behind you, to the left is the farm 'Atalix' but immediately turn right and go through another gate, follow the track round with the wall on your right, back towards the marsh; at the end of this field there is a pair of gates that are usually padlocked especially if there are pigs or cows in the field you have just passed through but it is possible to climb round over the wall if you are reasonably agile.

❸ Over the gates the track heads inland into the barranco (valley) at the head of the marsh past some wet pools on the right that attract Green Sandpipers; continue for about 300 m until you can turn right at a point where dwellings have been cut into the rock on the left, go through a gate, over a small bridge and across the valley. The valley here is another good area for Egyptian Vultures and Booted Eagle so linger and see what turns up.

Across the valley turn right and follow a track past an old farmhouse called Son Benet, go through another pair of gates and you can see the river 'Torrent de Son Boter' and the urbanisation of Son Bou ahead of you. Follow the track round over the river to the urbanisation ❹, turn right and make your way back to the car park by following the road nearest to the marsh so you can still bird on the way. The total round trip walking time is about three to four hours plus birding time but well worth the effort in such a superb area.

It is, of course, possible to cover this valley without having to climb the gates or walls at Atalix by following the directions in reverse from the western end of the Son Bou urbanisation.

Other Sites

Son Parc

Son Parc used to have an extensive reedbed but tourist development has fairly drastically reduced the area, however the beds still hold typical marsh species such as Great Reed Warbler, Reed Warbler and even a few Moustached Warbler as well as Fan-tailed and

29

Cetti's Warblers in the margins.

To get there take the Son Parc turning 4.4 km from the Fornells end of the PM 710 Mahon/ Fornells road and down to the Son Parc entrance, follow the road past the urbanisation and the Club Son Parc, which is zoned for more development, to the supermarket after 3.0 km. At the supermarket turn left signposted 'Playa' , to the left you will see the small reedbed, park down this road just before the beach and take a small track back to your left and scan over the reeds for typical marsh species.

Punta Nati

A headland on the extreme north-west point of the island, again a very barren and flat area and very hard underfoot.

To get there take the road north out of Ciutadella signposted 'Punta Nati'. The birds here are the same as can be seen at Punta de s'Escullar but it is possible to drive right to the point and view from the road for Thekla Lark, Short-toed Lark, Tawny Pipit and maybe Stone Curlew.

At the end of the road at the lighthouse, park and walk the short distance out onto the small headland which makes a good viewpoint for shearwaters and gulls; also don't forget to check the rubbish tip on the way for Red Kite, Egyptian Vulture and Raven, still worthwhile despite the commencement of burning which has dramatically reduced the numbers of birds now seen here.

Fornells

The Bahia de Fornells, east of the C723 road 6.0 km to 8.0 km north from Mercadal, is always worth checking for terns, and for waders at the small disused salt pans situated on the right at K6.5 before Fornells; there is no access to these pans, which are on private property, but they can be scanned quite adequately by telescope from the roadside where there is suitable parking.

Monte Toro

This is the highest point on the island but only 357 m high, nevertheless from here you get splendid views (see Plate 10) and it can be an ideal place to look for the raptors. Monte Toro is very close to Mercadal on the east side and is signposted from the town on the C723 Fornells road.

Mercadal Depuradora

There is a new depuradora 2.0 km north outside Mercadal on the Cala Pregonda/Binimel La road; the depuradora is a small one but it consists of open pans and has recently been constructed on a wet area, consequently it attracts waders and is well worth a short stop and scan on the way to Tirant and Cap de Cavalleria.

Cabo Menorca/Bajoli Lighthouse

Another area very similar to Punta Nati, this is the westernmost point of Menorca and is signposted from Ciutadella.

Isla de l'Aire

The Isla de l'Aire is situated off the south-east tip of Menorca and is the first landfall for migrants approaching Menorca in spring. There is no regular access but the local Menorcan ringing group regularly trap in spring and autumn with spectacular results; recent records include Orphean Warbler and Trumpeter Finch as well as Icterine and Melodious Warblers which always turn up more regularly in ringing campaigns on the off-islands than are found by birdwatching on the main islands.

Ibiza

Introduction Ibiza

Ibiza is a similar size to Menorca, 40.0 km by 21.0 km, but it is totally different in character being much brasher and noisier around the resorts; it is much quieter when you get out into the country birdwatching. The island is well wooded but interspersed with private houses and small farms inland so you can never completely get away from 'civilisation' on this island. Nonetheless the scenery is very beautiful, the island is higher than Menorca and has spectacular coastal cliffs, especially on the north coast, indented with attractive calas on all coasts, most of which have been developed with hotels and apartments for the tourist industry.

The island is as popular as Mallorca as a holiday destination and has been for as many years, consequently the tourist infrastructure has been in place a long time and there are many flights and holiday packages available direct to Ibiza from many UK airports during the holiday season.

It is possible to combine Ibiza with Mallorca for a two centre holiday as the islands are connected by air with regular flights throughout the day, and also by a daily car ferry, although the ferry trip is rather long and runs overnight fom Ibiza to Mallorca.

Birds in Ibiza and when to stay

Ibiza does not have the spectacular well known birding sites of Mallorca or even Menorca, but a birdwatching holiday can be well worthwhile provided one does not expect quite the variety of species or numbers to be found on Mallorca. Apart from the Salinas in the south there is no other main site and the island is therefore described mainly by area with a few specific sites detailed to guide the birder to the more accessible birding areas. It's closer proximity to the Spanish mainland, it is only 90.0 km away, does mean that some species not present or common on Mallorca are more plentiful here, the most notable being Rock Sparrow; there is also the probability of more migrant overshoots and expansion of range from the mainland, maybe even Trumpeter Finch in the course of time.

There are the typical Balearic resident specialities here such as Audouin's Gull, Black-winged Stilt, Kentish Plover, Hoopoe, Sardinian Warbler, Blue Rock Thrush, Wryneck and Thekla Lark and especially Marmora's Warbler, which are easier to see

31

here and would appear to be at a greater density than on Mallorca, as well as the fore mentioned Rock Sparrow although this species is much easier to see on Formentera.

The migration period is similar to the rest of the Balearics, therefore the best time to visit would be in mid April to early May when migration is at it's peak and waders can be seen on the salinas, as well as birds such as Bee-eater, Golden Oriole and even Roller passing through. Bee-eaters stay to breed occasionally if the conditions are right and there is suitable habitat that has not been altered or built over; Eleonora's Falcon also breed on the island and off-shore islands but not in the numbers on Mallorca. Autumn migration is slightly earlier here than on Mallorca and Menorca and may even be heavier.

Where to stay

With holiday resorts situated all around the coast the choice of where to stay is enormous but the birdwatcher would be better advised to stay fairly near to Ibiza town from where the salinas can be covered regularly, numerous ferries run every day to Formentera, and Audouin's Gull frequent the harbour. However Sant Antoni (San Antonio Abad) set on a beautiful inlet on the opposite coast, is just 15.0 km away and would also make a good centre for both family and birdwatcher. The rest of the resorts are mostly based on the developed calas, and access to the cliffs and woods either side are very restricted and in most cases impossible.

Food and shopping

There are many holiday apartments in Ibiza and self catering is very popular and makes a good choice for the birdwatcher allowing greater flexibility with meal times. Consequently in the coastal resorts there are numerous shops and supermarkets catering for this market and also many restaurants and bars for eating out, but, beware, the villages inland do not have the variety of bars offering tapas and snacks that are available on Mallorca.

Getting around

A car is essential for the birdwatcher on Ibiza as it is necessary to get out of the resorts and into the countryside to start your birdwatching. Car hire is readily available and reasonably cheap, the rules and regulations are the same as for the rest of the Balearics and the advice given in the Menorca section is the same for Ibiza.

Public transport is not really an option as, although the network between towns and resorts is good, you will be unable to stop where and when you want, and the remoter spots more suitable for birdwatching are not on the public transport routes. Cycling is also unlikely to be an option unless you are either very keen or in close proximity to the salinas in the south.

When exploring by car a lot of the side tracks eventually lead to private property but do not let that put you off exploring, unless you come to a private sign or padlocked gates, as many tracks near the coast, especially in the north, eventually reach lovely coastal areas away from the tourist calas where you can explore more freely. There are also many new tracks being bulldozed for new roads and these are also well worth exploring as they take you into virgin territory, at least until they have been developed and urbanised. Getting into the coastal habitat next to the calas is next to impossible, even on foot, so take advantage of these new tracks when you see them.

Weather and clothing

In summer it can be even hotter than on Mallorca and the winter is wetter, but in the prime birdwatching time of spring and autumn the weather can be mixed and the usual precaution of being prepared for all weather conditions from cool with rain to hot sun should be taken.

Crime
The same warning about theft from cars given for Menorca certainly applies here and probably more so when in the resorts, and the same applies to valuables in hotels.

Other general points
The money unit is the peseta and all resorts will have banks, open in the mornings, and hotels to exchange currency.

The native language here is Ibizencan, (yet another dialect of Catalan) but again all islanders speak Spanish (Castellano); English as well as German will be understood in all the tourist resorts.

Catalan names for towns and places are being used with greater frequency on the island I have therefore used these names in the text where appropriate despite referring to the island by it's well known Spanish name of Ibiza and not the Catalan 'Eivissa'.

As stated previously there are no poisonous snakes on the Balearics but mosquitoes may cause a problem at certain times of the year so take the precaution of using an insect repellent should you react to bites.

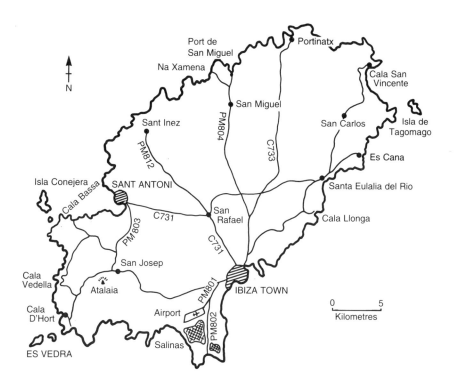

Map 9. The island of Ibiza, showing the principal roads, towns and birdwatching areas.

Birding sites on Ibiza

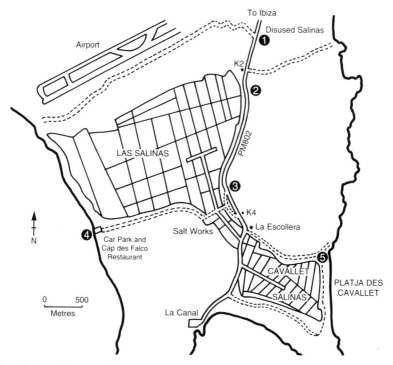

Map 10. Las Sainas and Cavellet Salinas, Ibiza.

Las Salinas (Salinera Espanola) and Cavallet Salinas (Map 10)

Las Salinas, situated to the southwest of Ibiza town and on the southern border of the airport, are the largest working salinas in the Balearics and the only wet area on Ibiza; consequently they are very attractive to waders on migration but due to disturbance from the works and close proximity of the airport they do not usually stay for any length of time. The same reasons account for the few birds that stay to breed, only Kentish Plover and a few pairs of Black-winged Stilt, although in recent years Shelduck have attempted to breed; Flamingos, however, find the salinas very attractive and in recent years have been seen in most months of the year with numbers sometimes reaching the eighties in the autumn and winter months.

To get there take the PM 801 road towards the airport and at the fork, 4.0 km out of Ibiza town just past San Jorge, take the PM 802 road signposted 'La Canal'.

❶ There is a track off to the right 1.5 km down this road that takes you to the back of the salinas on the north-east side, but access may be blocked due to the proximity of the airport.

To the left at this point there were some disused salinas on the left hand side, excellent for waders, but these have now virtually disappeared under motorcycle tracks and presumably for development in due course; however there are one or two wet areas remaining and they are well worth checking, turn left at K2.0 signposted 'Torre des Carregador', this is a mauve 'Concellar Ibiza y Formentera' sign, this track takes you towards the coast with the wet areas on your left .

34

Back on the main road the main salinas appear on your right just after K2.0 at the restaurant 'Positiv' ❷, check over the pans from this point in the morning with the sun behind you, there is a cycle track on the side of the road but be careful where you park as regards traffic.

❸ Access to the main salinas is 4.0 km down this road from the fork, there is a small track on the right signposted 'Cap Falco' and 'Cap des Falco Restaurante' with rustic signs. It is possible to drive down this track on the right, turning almost immediately right at a tee junction in the track, across the main saltworks access road and in front of the works then following the southern edge of the pans heading west to the coast. With the pans on your right and woods on your left; stop were you will and scan the pans for waders and terns, and the woods for warblers and other passerines. Be careful when parking to view the pans, this is a busy commercial operation so do not block access anywhere.

❹ At the end of this track, 1.5 km, there is the sea and a rustic restaurant with a turn around for cars, park here but it could be busy with restricted parking in high season, Plate 11 shows the view north from here.

From here there is unfortunately no access to the track heading north along the western edge of the salinas, but it is possible to walk north along the shingle bank of large stones to reach the northern end of the salinas; an area more favoured by Flamingos and waders as it is further away from the commercial activity and has more vegetation to the margins of the settling pans as opposed to the evaporation pans.

A short walk from the restaurant south on the cliffs towards Cabo Falco should produce Blue Rock Thrush, Thekla Lark and any passerine migrants that may be around.

Return to the PM 802 road by retracing your route and turning right at the tee junction in the track just before the road to get onto the road at K4.0, turn right and continue south for 100 m to the bar 'La Escollera', turn left here and follow this track to the beach, Platja des Cavallet; the pans on your right are an extension of the main salinas, the Playa Cavallet salinas, again scan the pans for waders and terns.

❺ From the beach car park it is possible to walk south on a path to the right of 'Bar Es Chiringuito' along the eastern edge of the pans with woods between you and the sea on your left-hand side. The path continues round the southern edge and it is possible to complete the circuit by returning via a track and the main road.

The west coast

The west coast area is generally flatter and more open than the rest of Ibiza but only comparatively so, there are still impressive cliffs and attractive calas on the coast and the highest points on Ibiza are in this area, the Atalaia de San Josep being the highest. The vegetation here is of mixed scrubland and pine woods interspersed with small Fincas (farms) in the south of the region, with the flatter areas to the north having more stony fields and open areas especially on the coast. There is no one special area that especially attracts birds or indeed birdwatchers so the technique is to explore the area by car stopping at suitable areas that attract your attention.

Atalaia de San Josep and Es Vedra

The highest point on the island and rising to 476 m, it is possible to drive to the top but a walk up the road makes a good birdwatching excursion.

To get there take the PM 803 road out of San Josep (San José) towards Sant Antoni, branch off left at K13.0 towards Cala Tarida/Cala Vedella, there are lots of unofficial signposts at this fork in the road including 'Cala Playa' 'Vedranella' 'Playa Cala Carbo' 'Playa Cala d'Hort' 'Hotel Club Aquarium' 'Talaia' and more; after 1.0 km there is a turn off to the left signposted 'Talaia', take this turn, which goes right to the top if you wish to drive, if you decide to walk park a little way up on the left at the first corner and proceed on foot towards the Atalaia birding all the way. On the lower slopes look out for the usual Mediterranean species including Hoopoe, Golden Oriole and even Roller; as you get higher and the trees get a little thinner look out for Marmora's Warblers here as well as the more expected Firecrest, Serin, Greenfinch and Crossbill. The road bends round the Atalaia ridge and affords stunning views over the surrounding countryside.

Returning to the road continue on towards Cala Tarida/Cala Vedella, where the road forks both roads are signposted 'Playa Cala Vedella' but take the left one which is also signposted 'Cala d'Hort'. A further 3.0 km on at a tee junction signposted 'Cala d'Hort turn left and 500 m up the hill turn right on a track signposted with a mauve sign 'Torre de Savinar'. The track is very rough so park a little way down and walk further on for a fabulous view of Es Vedra (Plate 12), an impressive island offshore together with sister island Es Vedranella, and home to a few pairs of Eleonora's Falcon in summer. The area around this spectacular viewpoint holds Marmora's Warbler as well as Blue Rock Thrush, Raven, Crag Martin, Peregrine, passerine migrants in season and in winter Black Redstart.

Returning to the road and turning left it is possible to continue north, via Cala Vedella, fairly close to the coast towards Cala Tarida; sandy areas on this route can attract Bee-eaters which have nested here in the past.

Past Cala Terida the second left turn takes you towards Cala Bassa, take the left fork approx. 1.0 km before Cala Bassa and continue to the coast, from here you can look out towards the Bledas Islands and Isla Conejera, this group of islands has breeding shearwaters and Shags. This headland area to the west of Cala Bassa is a good spot for migrants such as wheatears, pipits, wagtails and finches. A quarry on the road to Cala Bassa held a small Bee-eater colony in 1993 so it is worth checking this area.

Ibiza is comparatively unknown birdwise so anywhere on this west coast could produce interesting birds especially in spring and autumn on migration, explore and please report your sightings.

The north coast.

The north coast is the most spectacular and the least developed part of the island, mostly wooded with pines and Holm Oak and typical Mediterranean maquis vegetation of myrtle and cistus and quite dense and difficult to access, the trick is to explore the tracks heading to the cliff edge as and where you can find them. The cliffs here are precipitous so take care especially if exploring alone. The following sites are of easy access by car and will take you into the typical habitat.

Sant Inez

Drive to Sant Inez from either Sant Antoni, San Rafael or San Miguel; from Ibiza town take the C 731/PM 812-1 road towards Sant Antoni and turn right at San Rafael on the PM 812-1 road signposted 'Sant Inez'.

Turn left at the Bar Tienda Can Cosni, a road which soon deteriorates to a sandy but drivable track; continue on for 2.0 km, checking the fields on either side for Thekla Lark and pipits, until you reach a bend in the track with an obvious parking place just in the pine woods, park and explore the coastal woods and scrub up to the cliff edge and, of course, be careful, the views are spectacular but the cliffs drop sheer to the sea. Expect to see Peregrine, gulls and shearwaters from the cliffs as well as Blue Rock Thrush, Sardinian Warblers and other scrub birds.

Na Xamena

This is a small but spectacular cala which is famous for a well known and exclusive hotel, 'The Hacienda', perched right on the cliff edge. To get there take the PM 804 road from San Miguel towards Port de San Miguel, just after K14.0, approaching Port de San Miguel, take the turning on the left signposted 'La Hacienda'. Drive up to the Hotel Hacienda through a very attractive valley and pass through the stone entrance pillars of Na Xamena. At the hotel continue just past the hotel entrance and turn left immediately by the right-hand side of the hotel, the track is rough but passable by car, park on the right-hand bend about 150 m up without blocking anybody's entrance/exit.

The view over the cliff back towards the hotel is spectacular; here there is a short but very narrow path on the cliff side of the wall that takes you to a point overlooking the small inlet, again be very careful of the precipitous drops. From here you can look out for passing shearwaters and Shag, and scan the cliffs for Eleonora's Falcon and Peregrine as well as Blue Rock Thrush, Common and Pallid Swift, and probably Rock Sparrow.

Portinatx

Portinatx is a developed cala which is in the process of more development; it is the most northerly resort on the island and is at the northern end of the C733 road 29.0 km from Ibiza town; watch out for the Spanish system of crossing main roads, before San Joan you have to turn right to go across both lanes of traffic to turn left, which is where you want to go.

Approaching Portinatx at K27.0 continue straight on following 'Playa es Port' signs, in Portinatx turn right at the brown sign 'Cala den Serra'; this unmade road takes you out of the usual overdeveloped holiday cala into a very nice garigue and maquis area.

Because of the expanding development, new tracks have been bulldozed through virgin scrub to the east of the cala, it is possible at the moment to explore these new tracks on foot . At a fork in the unmade road take the left towards Cala den Serra and at a house on the left and a white building numbered 29 a bulldozed track on the left leads out to the headland, Punta Moscarate, and takes you right into Marmora's Warbler territory. There are numerous tracks in this area so take care not to lose your way.

Retrace your route to the fork in the unmade road, from here you can take the right fork signposted 'Sant Joan de Fabritja and 'San Vicente' and drive all the way to San Vicente in the extreme east of the island, BUT beware it is unmade most of the way and is a bit of a bone-shaking ride.

The east coast and south-east coast

The east coast has a couple of headlands that are well worth exploring, the one north of Cala San Vicente is difficult to access, but Cabo Roig, overlooking the island of Tagomago, can be reached via a minor road from San Carlos. This coast is very wild and undeveloped at present and the vegetation is much the same as the north coast.

In contrast the south-east coast is the most developed on the island apart from Sant Antoni, the calas are very attractive but over-developed, however there are one or two spots worth birding.

Santa Eulalia del Rio (Map 11)

Santa Eulalia del Rio, as it's name suggests, lies on a river, not very big but one of the very few in the Balearics. There is a small area of Phragmites reed-bed here, the only one on Ibiza, which is worth checking for migrant wetland species, the odd Reed and Great Reed Warbler as well as Fan-tailed Warbler and Cetti's Warbler.

To get there take the C 810 road west out of Santa Eulalia towards Ibiza crossing over the river and then immediately turn left on the coast road towards Cala Llonga, after 100 m turn left again at 'Hobby' and 'Siesta' signs painted on the pink walls of the 'Bar Rio Restaurant' ❶. About 500 m down this road there is a footpath on the left by a bridge that leads to the back of the small reedbed, take the first left after the bridge to 'Lola's' hairdressing salon ❷, go past 'Lola's' and park at the end. The small reedbed is on the left and from here you can scan for the wetland species.

From here you may be able to walk down to the river and cross over the small side stream by passing through a gap in the hedge and exploring the wasteland area next to the river ❸; the field to the north of the reedbed is fenced but if it is possible to get access to the north side of the reedbed walk up for a better view of the birds.

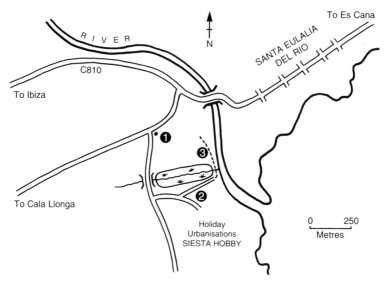

Map 11. Santa Eulalia del Rio, Ibiza.

Es Cana

Mentioned here as a possible source of a boat trip to Isla Tagomago. The island of Tagomago is a breeding site for Mediterranean Shearwater and possibly Eleonora's Falcon; well worth a trip round the island even if you cannot land.

Other sites

If you discover any boat trips that visit the other off-shore islands do try them as the birds will be relatively undisturbed compared to the main island if you can land, if not they will give you closer views of the seabirds. Try Sant Antoni for trips round the Bledas islands and Isla Conejera, and perhaps also to Isla Es Vedra; and try Ibiza town or Cala Vedella for trips to Isla Es Vedra.

Ibiza is comparatively unknown for birding so explore and try other sites, for example you can stop anywhere in the centre of the island and immediately see Thekla Lark and even Rock Sparrow by a main road, but information on birds such as Woodchat Shrike would be of interest.

Formentera

Introduction Formentera

Formentera is a small narrow island only 20.0 km by road from west to east and it is only 4.0 km south of Ibiza to Isla Espalmador, although the boat trip from Ibiza harbour to La Savina is 24.0 km. Composed of fossil coral reef with few areas of trees it offers a flat and barren landscape, especially on the two capes of Barbaria and La Mola, but it has superb beaches and possesses a charm all of it's own, it is very reminiscent of a Caribbean island and is one of the author's favourite islands. Formentera is famous for it's Savina Pine, a Juniper which grows very slowly here and is very hard and dense, it is used for a variety of purposes such as boat slipways and supports for patio roofs both on Ibiza and Formentera.

The only access to the island is by boat with ferries from at least two different companies sailing at regular intervals throughout the day from Ibiza town, including at least one per day capable of ferrying cars; consequently with no airport it is somewhat less frenetic with holiday makers and the pace here is definitely slower, even slower than on Menorca. The best areas can be covered in a day and birdwatching day trips are possible from Ibiza, however Formentera is well worth a weeks ornithological exploration on it's own, certainly in spring or autumn, so all the best sites are documented.

Birds on Formentera and when to stay

Formentera, although very small, is easier to cover and is altogether better for birding than Ibiza, it also has the best site in the Pitiusas, the Estany Pudent, a large lake and adjoining salinas which attract migrant waders in spring and autumn and a large flock of Black-necked Grebe as well as duck in winter. The resident species on the island include Shag, Peregrine Falcon, Black-winged Stilt, Kentish Plover, Hoopoe, Thekla Lark, Blue Rock Thrush, Sardinian Warbler, Marmora's Warbler and Rock Sparrow in good numbers. Summer visitors include Short-toed Lark, Tawny Pipit, Spotted Flycatcher, Turtle Dove and Woodchat Shrike.

The best time to visit is in spring when migrants are passing through the island and again, due to it's closer proximity to the mainland, almost anything can turn up here.

The island is also very important for it's breeding colonies of Mediterranean Shearwater, in far greater numbers here than anywhere else in the Balearics; the same applies to Storm Petrel which breed on the islets between Formentera and Ibiza. The largest colony of Audouin's Gull is also on one of these islets.

Where to stay

The one big tourist area is at Es Pujols with the expected hotels and self-catering apartments; the port of La Savina also has hotels and apartments but the island is so small it really does not matter where you stay although both Es Pujols and La Savina are close to the Estany Pudent area which is the main birdwatching site on the island. There are other small tourist developments in other parts of the island but these are farther away from the prime site of Estany Pudent.

Food and shopping

With many self catering apartments available the main centres of La Savina, Es Pujols, Sant Francesc Xavier (San Francisco Javier) and Sant Ferran (San Fernando) have modern supermarkets open between 8.00 am and 1.00 pm and 4.00 pm to 8.00 pm, and there are various superb restaurants and bars near all the beaches and calas as well as in the one resort and the three small towns.

Getting around

Walking is possible if concentrating in the west of the island but bicycling using a mountain bike is the ideal, not because there are any hills, but because there are many tracks which are narrow and stony and totally unsuitable for cars. Car hire is available but not necessary on this island unless you wish to frequently visit La Mola and Cap de Barbaria or wish to cover everywhere in a day. There are many places that hire bicycles, or if you prefer, mopeds, also ideal but noisy.

If you are not keen on cycling it is possible to get a local bus from one end of the island to the other, ideal if you wish to get to the La Mola end of the island. There is an excellent map of the island, available only on the island and simply called 'Mapa de Formentera', it is recommended that you buy it as it accurately details ALL the tracks on the island.

Weather and climate

Hot and almost tropical in summer, wet and very windy in winter. As usual in the western Mediterranean the spring and autumn can be changeable so take the usual precautions of waterproofs and woollies as well as the shorts and suntan lotion.

Crime

The same warning about theft from cars given for Menorca and Ibiza will apply here also, certainly when in the resort, and the same warning applies to valuables left in hotels.

Other general points

The money unit is the peseta and all resorts will have banks, open in the mornings, and hotels to exchange currency.

The native language here is Ibizencan, (yet another dialect of Catalan) but again all islanders speak Spanish (Castellano) and English as well as German will be understood in all the tourist resorts.

As stated before there are no poisonous snakes on the Balearics but mosquitoes may cause a problem at certain times of the year so take the precaution of using an insect repellent should you react to bites.

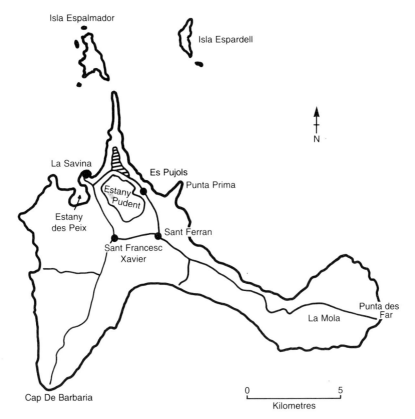

Map 12. The island of Formentera showing the principal roads, towns and birdwatching sites.

Birding sites on Formentera

Estany Pudent and Salinas Marroig and Ferrer (Map 13)

This area is the single best birdwatching site in the Pitiusas consisting of a large brackish lake, Estany Pudent (literally 'smelly lagoon' which does at times smell) and the adjacent salinas, 'Salinas Marroig' and the smaller 'Salinas Ferrer'.

The road from La Savina to Es Pujols skirts the northern and eastern edges of the lake and this side is easily covered by car; however to cover the lagoon and surrounding area thoroughly, use a bicycle, or walk, on the track skirting the western and southern sides of the lagoon as well.

In the morning it is best to start from Es Pujols as the sun will be behind you; just out of Es Pujols on the La Savina road take the track on the left by a bar/cafe ❶, this will give good views over the southern portion of the lake and from here you should be able to spot the flock of Black-necked Grebes, which has numbered up to 3,000 in winter in past years but now attracts only about 300, but even in high summer more than 100 non-breeding adults can be present. This track is closed to cars but is easily traversed by bicycle; plate 13 shows the view from this point.

Do not forget to scan the scrub area to the south and west of this track, it is good for passerines especially all the usual scrub warblers including Marmora's.

41

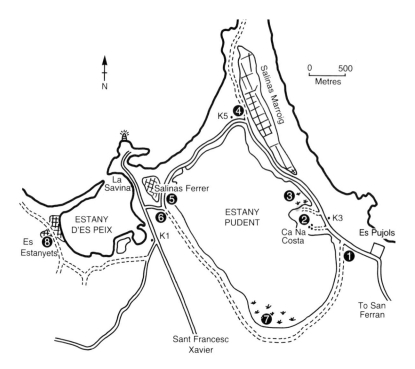

Map 13. Estany Pudent and Estany d'es Peix, Formentera.

Retrace your route and continue on the main road towards La Savina for approx. 0.5 km until you come to a small promontory with a signpost 'Sepulcre megalitic Ca Na Costa' ❷; take the track on the left hand side for 200 m up to this megalith, park and from here it is possible to skirt round through the scrub until you can once again overlook the lake. This vantage point is higher than the surrounding land and gives excellent views over the lake where you can scan for waders and terns as well as for the grebes.

❸ To the northern side of this promontory there is a marshy area by the lake which is a good spot for waders reached by another track off the road on the left.

Return again to the road and continuing on a little further will bring you to the start of the Salinas Marroig on the right hand side; stop and scan the salt pans for gulls, terns and maybe the odd flock of Flamingos.

❹ A further 1.0 km on there is a sandy track off to the right signposted 'Playa beach Illyetas, Bar Restaurante es Moli de Sal', passable by cars, this track follows the rest of these salt pans and continues on to the Platja de Llevant; continue to scan the pans for waders and the dunes further on for typical open habitat species such as Short-toed Lark and Tawny Pipit as well as migrant wheatears and chats. Beware there are 22 concrete Flamingos on these pans, you are not allowed to tick them unless they fly.

Return to the road and continue along the north shore of the lake for another 1.5 km until you come to the 'Salinas Ferrer' on the right ❺, scan these smaller pans also for waders and terns, then continue the short distance to where there is a track off to the left ❻ which follows the west shore of the lake. Again this track, which continues round to near Es Pujols ❶, is closed to cars but is easily passable by bicycle and passes a small

42

reed bed **❼** at the southern end which should be checked for Reed and Great Reed
Warblers and crakes. It is best to do this western part of the track in the afternoon when
the sun will be behind you.

Of course you can do this trip in the reverse direction if you so wish and are staying at
La Savina or just visiting on a day trip. In which case, just leaving La Savina take the
first left at the signpost 'Es Pujols 4.4 km, 6.3 km to Sant Ferran', the Estany Pudent
will be on your right almost immediately.

Estany des Peix and Es Estanyets (Map 13)

This lagoon is open to the sea and is therefore not so attractive to waders as Estany
Pudent, but terns are regular and if birding in early spring, well worth scanning for duck;
the small disused salinas, Es Estanyets, at the western end of the lagoon are however
well worth a look for waders.

Situated on the west side of La Savina this lagoon is easily viewed from the town
itself. To cover the southern and western sides take the right turn at K1.0 out of La
Savina and then the first track on the right after 400 m by the first house just after the
lagoon. This sandy track is passable by car but quite exciting for those used to wide
tarmac dual carriage-ways, just follow round the edge of the lagoon keeping right at
junctions and you should come out onto a wider area overlooking the Es Estanyets
disused salinas (Plate 14) at **❽**.

Cap de Barbaria

The Cap de Barbaria peninsular is the most southerly point of the Balearics and
therefore the nearest point to north Africa. To get there take the right turn at 3.1km from
La Savina in the town of Sant Francesc Xavier signposted 'Far des Cap de Barbaria'.
This road is 9.0 km long and passes through some very attractive wooded areas and it is
well worth stopping and birding at various spots down this road before emerging onto
the very barren point of Es Pla del Rei (Plate 15).

The area is the first landfall for passerines in spring and the last in autumn, and is full
of Wheatears, Yellow Wagtails,Pipits and Whinchats at these times and therefore well
worth checking for rarer migrants; residents such as Red-legged Partridge, Thekla Lark,
and Blue Rock Thrush are also present. The lighthouse at the southernmost tip is a good
spot for sea-watching for Cory's and Mediterranean Shearwaters as well as looking out
for Peregrines and Kestrels. The woods prior to the point attract Flycatchers and
Nightingales as well as Woodchat Shrikes. Despite the proximity of the La Mola
Peninsular it is possible to get a fall of migrants here and not at La Mola and, of course,
vice versa.

La Mola

La Mola is another barren headland situated at the extreme east of the island 20.0 km
from La Savina, but the cliffs are slightly higher here than at Cap de Barbaria. To get
there follow the main road east across the narrow isthmus through Es Calo and up onto
the La Mola peninsular, wooded at first before emerging to barren ground after the
village of El Pilar; continue right to the end at the lighthouse, the 'Punta des Far'. Park
here and explore the cliffs to the north and south of the lighthouse; this is the best area
for looking out for Cory's and Mediterranean Shearwater as well as Peregrine Falcon
which frequent all these cliffs.

About 0.5 km to the north of the lighthouse there is a small gorge (see Plate 16) that
is home to a flock of 20 Rock Sparrows, in fact this whole area is prime territory for
Rock Sparrow as well as Thekla Lark, Tawny Pipit and Cirl Bunting, and is another
prime site for migrants.

Other areas

Punta Prima

Situated to the east of Es Pujols and north of Sant Ferran this area and the cliffs to the south is another area of spectacular coastal scenery best explored by bicycle and on foot. Access is via a track on the right at K1.0 out of Sant Ferran towards Es Pujols. Walking along the coast should produce more Rock Sparrow as well as Tawny Pipit and Cirl Bunting; Peregrine also breed here as well as Mediterranean Shag.

The beaches

To the north 'Platja de Tramuntana' and to the south 'Platja de Migjorn' these beaches to the north and south of the isthmus are long and sandy, the bird interest being in the immediate hinterland during spring when passerine migrants should be looked for at the back of the beach.

Isla Espalmador and Isla Espardel

These are two islands situated just north of Formentera between Formentera and Ibiza; there is no regular access to these islands but should the chance of a boat trip arise it should be taken just for the experience although the birds to be found on these islands are the same as on Formentera, but there is always the chance of migrants both waders on the shore and passerines in the scrub and low trees.

Flora and Fauna of Menorca, Ibiza and Formentera

Apart from the birds, Menorca especially is also very popular with the flower hunters, this is due to the considerable number of endemic species found here, typical of a remote Mediterranean island, as well as a good selection of Mediterranean orchids and other typical Mediterranean flora.

The best time to come looking at the flowers is from late March to late April and this also applies to the Pitiusas which despite not having quite the profusion of Menorca do have a good selection of typical Mediterranean plants and flowers.

This is not the book to even attempt to list the flowers but we can recommend using Mediterranean Wild Flowers by Marjory Blamey.

In common with the main island of Mallorca the rest of the Balearics lost all their large mammals early in man's colonisation of the islands, today we are left with some of the smaller mammals such as Rabbit, Hare, the North African sub-species of Hedgehog, rats and mice and maybe the odd Weasel; various species of bats are found on these islands but their status on each is very little known.

Being islands well out into the Mediterranean various species of Dolphin and Whales are regularly recorded and even the very occasional Loggerhead Turtle can be seen from any good vantage point on the cliffs and occasionally unfortunately washed up dead on the shore.

Reptiles and Amphibians are poorly represented compared to other Mediterranean islands but Menorca is the most prolific of the Balearics with Green Toad, Marsh frog and also Stripeless Tree Frog, both Moorish Gecko and Turkish Gecko of which a striped population occurs on Menorca, and three species of lizard, the Balearic endemic Lilford's Wall Lizard, Italian Wall Lizard and Moroccan Wall Lizard.

The Pitiusas on the other hand only have the endemic Ibiza Wall Lizard apart from the Geckos and Marsh Frog.

Two species of Tortoise both Hermann's and Spur-thighed occur on the islands, and snakes are represented by Viperine Snake, Grass Snake (probably only at Son Bou, Menorca), False Smooth Snake and Ladder Snake, the latter again only found on Menorca.

Butterflies and Moths are reasonably well represented on these offshore islands with Swallowtail, Cleopatra, Painted Lady, Bath White, Speckled Wood, Clouded Yellow and a variety of 'blues' including Lang's Short-tailed Blue usually in evidence in season and very often in profusion; the list is, of course, much longer and includes spectacular species such as Two-tailed Pasha, an immigrant from North Africa.

Moths are also well represented including some of the spectacular Hawk moths such as Hummingbird Hawk Moth, Oleander Hawk Moth and even occasionally Deaths Head.

There is also a good selection of dragonflies and damselflies in the wet areas, and hymenoptera, beetles etc.; certainly enough for the most dedicated naturalist.

References

Blamey, M. & Grey-Wilson,C. 1993. Mediterranean Wild Flowers. Harper-Collins London.
Hearl, G. &King, J. A Birdwatching Guide to Mallorca. Arlequin Press, Chelmsford.
King, J.R. & Hearl, G.C. in prep. Birds of the Balearic Islands. T. & A.D. Poyser, London.
Arnold E.N. & Burton J.A. 1978. A Field Guide to the Reptiles and Amphibians of Britain and Europe. Collins, Glasgow.

Check list of the birds of Menorca and the Pitiusas

This list includes most species that have been recorded in Menorca and the Pitiusas for which there is adequate documentation. The order follows that of Voous and the chosen English names are those preferred by the author.

The status codes used are defined below but it should be remembered that the codes are greatly simplified and it is possible to find winter visitors staying on into late spring and even summer or vice versa. Where the status varies between Menorca, Eivissa (Ibiza) and Formentera the status code is followed by the initials for the island in brackets e.g Rock Sparrow V (Me) R (Ei &Fo); where the bird does not occur on any one island, only the initials for the island it occurrs on are given, and where the status is similar on all the islands no island initials are used.

For species marked as vagrants V, all records should be accompanied by a description for the local records committee, whilst those marked V* are national rarities, and records are considered by the CIR, the Iberian Rarities Committee.

Species not listed here but observed on the islands are vagrants or escapes and records should be accompanied with full details and descriptions.

Details of all records submitted to the author will be forwarded to the relevant authorities.

R	Resident	RM	Rare Migrant
S	Summer	V	Vagrant
W	Winter	?	Status requiring clarification
M	Migrant		

46

English name	Scientific name	Status
Red-throated Diver	*Gavia stellata*	V
Black-throated Diver	*Gavia arctica*	V
Great Northern Diver	*Gavia immer*	V
Little Grebe	*Tachybaptus ruficollis*	R (Me) W (Fo)
Great Crested Grebe	*Podiceps cristatus*	W
Red-necked Grebe	*Podiceps grisegena*	V
Slavonian Grebe	*Podiceps auritus*	V*
Black-necked Grebe	*Podiceps nigricollis*	R? (Fo) W, M (Me &Ei)
Cory's Shearwater	*Calonectris diomeda*	R
Mediterranean Shearwater	*Puffinus yelkouan*	R
Storm Petrel	*Hydrobates pelagicus*	S
Gannet	*Sula bassana*	RM
Cormorant	*Phalacrocorax carbo*	W
Shag	*Phalacrocorax aristotelis*	R
Bittern	*Botaurus stellaris*	RM
Little Bittern	*Ixobrychus minutus*	M,S? (Me) M (Ei&Fo)
Night Heron	*Nycticorax nycticorax*	M
Squacco Heron	*Ardeola ralloides*	M
Cattle Egret	*Bubulcus ibis*	W
Little Egret	*Egretta garzetta*	M,R?
Great White Egret	*Egretta alba*	W(Me)
Grey Heron	*Ardea cinerea*	W
Purple Heron	*Ardea purpurea*	S? (Me) M
Black Stork	*Ciconia nigra*	RM
White Stork	*Ciconia ciconia*	RM
Glossy Ibis	*Plegadis falcinellus*	RM (Me) V (Ei&Fo)
Spoonbill	*Platalea leucorodia*	RM
Greater Flamingo	*Phoenicopterus ruber*	M (Me), W (Ei) RM (Me &Fo)
Mute Swan	*Cygnus olor*	V*
Greylag Goose	*Anser anser*	W
Ruddy Shelduck	*Tadorna ferruginea*	V*
Shelduck	*Tadorna tadorna*	RM, S?(Ei)
Wigeon	*Anas penelope*	W
Gadwall	*Anas strepera*	W
Teal	*Anas crecca*	W
Blue-winged Teal	*Anas discors*	V* (Me)
Mallard	*Anas platyrhynchos*	W,M
Pintail	*Anas acuta*	W,M (Me) M (Ei&Fo)
Garganey	*Anas querquedula*	M,W (Me) M (Ei&Fo)
Shoveler	*Anas clypeata*	W,M (Me) M (Ei&Fo)
Marbled Teal	*Marmaronetta angustirostris*	V
Red-crested Pochard	*Netta rufina*	V (Me&Fo)
Pochard	*Aythya ferina*	M,W

English name	Scientific name	Status
Ferruginous Duck	*Aythya nyroca*	RM
Tufted Duck	*Aythya fuligula*	W(Me),V(Ei&Fo)
Scaup	*Aythya marila*	V
Common Eider	*Somateria mollissima*	V (Me)
Common Scoter	*Melanitta nigra*	V (Fo)
Velvet Scoter	*Melanitta fusca*	V (Me)
Goldeneye	*Bucephala clangula*	V (Me)
Red-breasted Merganser	*Mergus serrator*	V (Me)
Honey Buzzard	*Pernis aviporus*	M
Black Kite	*Milvus migrans*	M
Red Kite	*Milvus milvus*	R (Me)M (Ei&Fo)
Egyptian Vulture	*Neophron percnopterus*	R (Me) V(Ei&Fo)
Black Vulture	*Aegypius monachus*	V (Me)
Short-toed Eagle	*Circaetus gallicus*	RM (Me) V (Ei&Fo)
Marsh Harrier	*Circus aeruginosus*	W,M (Me) M (Ei&Fo)
Hen Harrier	*Circus cyaneus*	W,M
Montagu's Harrier	*Circus pygargus*	M
Sparrowhawk	*Accipiter nisus*	W(Me)M(Ei&Fo)
Common Buzzard	*Buteo buteo*	M
Booted Eagle	*Hieraaetus pennatus*	R(Me) M(Ei&Fo)
Bonelli's Eagle	*Hieraaetus fasciatus*	V
Osprey	*Pandion haliaetus*	R(Me) M(Ei&Fo)
Lesser Kestrel	*Falco naumanni*	V (Me)
Kestrel	*Falco tinnunculus*	R
Red-footed Falcon	*Falco vespertinus*	M (Me) RM (Ei&Fo)
Merlin	*Falco columbarius*	V
Hobby	*Falco subbuteo*	RM
Eleonora's Falcon	*Falco eleonorae*	S(Ei) M(Me&Fo)
Lanner	*Falco biarmicus*	V
Peregrine	*Falco peregrinus*	R
Red-legged Partridge	*Alectoris rufa*	R
Quail	*Coturnix coturnix*	R(Me) M(Ei&Fo)
Andalusian Hemipode	*Turnix sylvatica*	V*(Fo)
Water Rail	*Rallus aquaticus*	R
Spotted Crake	*Porzana porzana*	W? (Me)
Little Crake	*Porzana parva*	V
Baillon's Crake	*Porzana pusilla*	V
Corncrake	*Crex crex*	V (Me)
Moorhen	*Gallinula chloropus*	R
Coot	*Fulica atra*	R
Common Crane	*Grus grus*	RM
Oystercatcher	*Haematopus ostralegus*	RM
Black-winged Stilt	*Himantopus himantopus*	S
Avocet	*Recurvirostra avosetta*	M
Stone Curlew	*Burhinus oedicnemus*	R(Me) RM(Ei&Fo)
Collared Pratincole	*Glareola pratincola*	M

English name	Scientific name	Status
Little Ringed Plover	*Charadrius dubius*	S (Me) M (Ei&Fo)
Ringed Plover	*Charadrius hiaticula*	M,W
Kentish Plover	*Charadrius alexandrinus*	R(Ei&Fo) M(Me)
Dotterel	*Charadrius morinellus*	V
Golden Plover	*Pluvialis apricaria*	W
Grey Plover	*Pluvialis squatarola*	W
Lapwing	*Vanellus vanellus*	W
Knot	*Calidris canutus*	RM
Sanderling	*Calidris alba*	RM
Little Stint	*Calidris minuta*	M,W (Ei&Fo) M (Me)
Temminck's Stint	*Calidris temminckii*	RM
Curlew Sandpiper	*Calidris ferruginea*	M (Me&Fo)
Purple Sandpiper	*Calidris maritima*	V (Me&Fo)
Dunlin	*Calidris alpina*	M,W
Ruff	*Philomachus pugnax*	M,W
Jack Snipe	*Lymnocryptes minimus*	W
Snipe	*Gallinago gallinago*	W
Woodcock	*Scolopax rusticola*	W
Black-tailed Godwit	*Limosa limosa*	M
Bar-tailed Godwit	*Limosa lapponica*	RM
Whimbrel	*Numenius phaeopus*	M
Curlew	*Numenius arquata*	W
Spotted Redshank	*Tringa erythropus*	M,W
Redshank	*Tringa totanus*	M,W
Marsh Sandpiper	*Tringa stagnatilis*	M
Greenshank	*Tringa nebularia*	M
Green Sandpiper	*Tringa ochropus*	M,W
Wood Sandpiper	*Tringa glareola*	M
Common Sandpiper	*Actitis hypoleucos*	M
Turnstone	*Arenaria interpres*	RM
Arctic Skua	*Stercorarius parasiticus*	V
Great Skua	*Stercorarius skua*	V
Mediterranean Gull	*Larus melanocephalus*	RM
Little Gull	*Larus minutus*	RM
Black-headed Gull	*Larus ridibundus*	M
Slender-billed Gull	*Larus genei*	RM
Audouin's Gull	*Larus audouinii*	R
Common Gull	*Larus canus*	V (Fo)
Lesser Black-backed Gull	*Larus fuscus*	RM
Yellow-legged Gull	*Larus cachinnans*	R
Great Black-backed Gull	*Larus marinus*	V(Fo)
Kittiwake	*Rissa tridactyla*	V(Fo)
Gull-billed Tern	*Gelochelidon niloctica*	RM
Caspian Tern	*Sterna caspia*	V
Sandwich Tern	*Sterna sandvicensis*	W,M
Common Tern	*Sterna hirundo*	V
Little Tern	*Sterna albifrons*	RM(Me&Fo)
Whiskered Tern	*Chlidonias hybridus*	M
Black Tern	*Chlidonias niger*	M

English name	Scientific name	Status
White-winged Black Tern	*Chlidonias leucopterus*	M
Guillemot	*Uria aalge*	V
Razorbill	*Alca torda*	V
Puffin	*Fratercula arctica*	W
Rock Dove	*Columba livia*	R (Me) W? (Ei&Fo)
Stock Dove	*Columba oenas*	V
Woodpigeon	*Columba palumbus*	R
Turtle Dove	*Streptopelia turtur*	S
Great Spotted Cuckoo	*Clamator glandarius*	V
Cuckoo	*Cuculus canorus*	S
Barn Owl	*Tyto alba*	R
Scops Owl	*Otus scops*	R
Little Owl	*Athene noctua*	R?(Me)V(Ei&Fo)
Long-eared Owl	*Asio otus*	R
Short-eared Owl	*Asio flammeus*	RM
Nightjar	*Caprimulgus europus*	M,S?
Swift	*Apus apus*	M,S
Pallid Swift	*Apus pallidu*	S
Alpine Swift	*Apus melba*	S(Me) M,S?(Ei&Fo)
Kingfisher	*Alcedo atthis*	W
Bee-eater	*Merops apiaster*	S
Roller	*Coracias garrulus*	RM
Hoopoe	*Upupa epops*	R
Wryneck	*Jynx torquilla*	M,W,R(Ei?)
Great Spotted Woodpecker	*Dendrocopos major*	V (Fo)
Short-toed Lark	*Calandrella brachydactyla*	S
Thekla Lark	*Galerida theklae*	R
Skylark	*Alauda arvensis*	W
Sand Martin	*Riparia riparia*	M
Crag Martin	*Ptyonoprogne rupestris*	M,W?
Swallow	*Hirundo rustica*	S
Red-rumped Swallow	*Hirundo daurica*	M
House Martin	*Delichon urbica*	S
Richard's Pipit	*Anthus novaeseelandiae*	V*
Tawny Pipit	*Anthus campestris*	S
Tree Pipit	*Anthus trivialis*	M
Meadow Pipit	*Anthus pratensis*	W
Red-throated Pipit	*Anthus cervinus*	RM
Water Pipit	*Anthus spinoletta*	W
Yellow Wagtail	*Motacilla flava*	S,M
Grey Wagtail	*Motacilla cinerea*	W
White Wagtail	*Motacilla alba*	W
Wren	*Troglodytes troglodytes*	R(Ei&Fo) W(Me)
Dunnock	*Prunella modularis*	W
Alpine Accentor	*Prunella collaris*	W(Me) V(Ei&Fo)
Rufous Bush Robin	*Cercotrichas galactotes*	V
Robin	*Erithacus rubecula*	W

English name	Scientific name	Status
Nightingale	*Luscinia megarhynchos*	S
Bluethroat	*Luscinia svecica*	W
Black Redstart	*Phoenicurus ochrurus*	W
Redstart	*Phoenicurus phoenicurus*	M
Whinchat	*Saxicola rubetra*	M
Stonechat	*Saxicola torquata*	R
Northern Wheatear	*Oenanthe oenanthe*	S(Ei&Fo) M(Me)
Black-eared Wheatear	*Oenanthe hispanica*	M
Black Wheatear	*Oenanthe leucura*	V(Me)
Rock Thrush	*Monticola saxatilis*	M
Blue Rock Thrush	*Monticola solitarius*	R
Ring Ouzel	*Turdus torquatus*	RM
Blackbird	*Turdus merula*	R
Fieldfare	*Turdus pilaris*	W
Song Thrush	*Turdus philomelos*	W
Redwing	*Turdus iliacus*	W
Mistle Thrush	*Turdus viscivorus*	W
Cetti's Warbler	*Cettia cetti*	R (Me)
Fan-tailed Warbler	*Cisticola juncidis*	R
Grasshopper Warbler	*Locustella naevia*	RM
Savi's Warbler	*Locustella luscinioides*	V
Moustached Warbler	*Acrocephalus melanopogon*	S (Me) RM (Ei&Fo)
Aquatic Warbler	*Acrocephalus paludicola*	V
Sedge Warbler	*Acrocephalus schoenobaenus*	RM
Marsh Warbler	*Acrocephalus palustris*	V
Reed Warbler	*Acrocephalus scirpaceus*	S(Me) S?(Ei)
Great Reed Warbler	*Acrocephalus arundinaceus*	S(Me) M(Ei&Fo)
Olivaceous Warbler	*Hippolais pallida*	RM (Ei&Fo)
Olive-tree Warbler	*Hippolais olivetorum*	V* (Fo)
Icterine Warbler	*Hippolais icterina*	M
Melodious Warbler	*Hippolais polyglotta*	M
Marmora's Warbler	*Sylvia sarda*	R (Ei&Fo)
Dartford Warbler	*Sylvia undata*	R(Me)RM(Ei&Fo)
Spectacled Warbler	Sylvia conspicillata	S
Subalpine Warbler	Sylvia cantillans	S(Me) M(Ei&Fo)
Sardinian Warbler	Sylvia melanocephala	R
Orphean Warbler	*Sylvia hortensis*	V
Barred Warbler	*Sylvia nisoria*	V*(Me&Fo)
Lesser Whitethroat	*Sylvia curruca*	V
Whitethroat	*Sylvia communis*	M
Garden Warbler	*Sylvia borin*	M
Blackcap	*Sylvia atricapilla*	R(Me&Ei) W(Fo)
Yellow-browed Warbler	*Phylloscopus inornatus*	V* (Me)
Bonelli's Warbler	*Phylloscopus bonelli*	M
Wood Warbler	*Phylloscopus sibilatrix*	M
Chiffchaff	*Phylloscopus collybita*	W
Willow Warbler	*Phylloscopus trochilus*	M
Goldcrest	*Regulus regulus*	W
Firecrest	*Regulus ignicapillus*	R

English name	Scientific name	Status
Spotted Flycatcher	*Muscicapa striata*	S
Red-breasted Flycatcher	*Ficedula parva*	V*(Me)
Collared Flycatcher	*Ficedula albicollis*	V*(Me)
Pied Flycatcher	*Ficedula hypoleuca*	M
Coal Tit	*Parus ater*	V (Ei)
Blue Tit	*Parus caeruleus*	V(Ei)
Great Tit	*Parus major*	R
Wallcreeper	*Trichodoma muraria*	V
Penduline Tit	*Remiz pendulinus*	W(Me) V(Ei&Fo)
Golden Oriole	*Oriolus oriolus*	M
Red-backed Shrike	*Lanius collurio*	RM
Great Grey Shrike	*Lanius excubitor*	V
Woodchat Shrike	*Lanius senator*	S
Alpine Chough	*Pyrrhocorax graculus*	V
Chough	*Pyrrhocorax pyrrhocorax*	V
Raven	*Corvus corax*	R
Starling	*Sturnus vulgaris*	W
Spotless Starling	*Sturnus unicolor*	RM
House Sparrow	*Passer domesticus*	R
Spanish Sparrow	*Passer hispaniolensis*	V
Tree Sparrow	*Passer montanus*	R(Ei) RM(Me)
Rock Sparrow	*Petronia petronia*	R(Ei&Fo) V(Me)
Snow Finch	*Montifringilla nivalis*	V(Me)
Chaffinch	*Fringilla coelebs*	R(Me) W(Ei&Fo)
Brambling	*Fringilla montifringilla*	RM
Serin	*Serinus serinus*	R(Ei) W(Fo&Me)
Citril Finch	*Serinus citrinella*	V(Me)
Greenfinch	*Carduelis chloris*	R
Goldfinch	*Carduelis carduelis*	R
Siskin	*Carduelis spinus*	W
Linnet	*Carduelis cannabina*	R
Crossbill	*Loxia curvirostra*	RM?,V?
Trumpeter Finch	*Bucanetes githagineus*	V
Bullfinch	*Pyrrhula pyrrhula*	V(Me&Fo)
Hawfinch	*Coccothraustes coccothraustes*	W,M
Yellowhammer	*Emberiza citrinella*	V(Fo)
Cirl Bunting	*Emberiza cirlus*	R?
Rock Bunting	*Emberiza cia*	V (Fo)
Ortolan Bunting	*Emberiza hortulana*	M
Reed Bunting	*Emberiza schoeniclus*	W
Corn Bunting	*Miliaria calandra*	R

					English name	Scientific name	Status

NOTES

NOTES

Forthcoming from T & A D Poyser

The Birds of the Balearic Islands

BY JON R KING AND GRAHAM HEARL

The Balearic Islands have long been a mecca for British and European bird watchers, combining superb scenery with a variety of mediterranean species. In this book, two experts on these islands give an overview of their ecology and avifauna, followed by species by species accounts with full notes on range, status and biology in the region. The volume follows the successful format of Birds in Scotland, Wales and Ireland and features dozens of evocative illustrations by John Busby.

For Publication Spring 1997   Price TBA   Hardback   ISBN: 085661-084-4

If you would like further information about this title please contact:
**T & A D Poyser, Marketing Department, 24-28 Oval Road, London NW1 7DX
Fax: (0)171 267 0362**